Growing God's Fruit

by G.H. Servant

WestBow Press books may be ordered through booksellers or by contacting:

WestBow Press
A Division of Thomas Nelson & Zondervan
1663 Liberty Drive
Bloomington, IN 47403
www.westbowpress.com
844-714-3454

ISBN: 979-8-3850-0362-4 (sc)
ISBN: 979-8-3850-0363-1 (e)

Library of Congress Control Number: 2023913810

Print information available on the last page.

WestBow Press rev. date: 09/05/2023

WESTBOW
PRESS®
A DIVISION OF THOMAS NELSON
& ZONDERVAN

LOVE

JOY

PEACE

SELF-CONTROL

KINDNESS

GENTLENESS

GOODNESS

"The wisdom in the scriptures and text, along with the activities and the object lesson at the end of the book, are enlightening and instructive as a family read or to enrich a Sunday school curriculum. Growing God's Fruit is a great conversation starter for adults and young people relating key scriptures to a terrific metaphor."

Pastor Frank H. Dobos

"As a parent, I believe it is so important for children to be guided and supported in their faith journey. That is why I consider learning about the fruits of the Spirit essential in helping children understand the "why" and "how" to make God-centered choices in their lives and how growing in these fruits also shapes and builds their character. *Growing God's Fruit* imparts this important learning and guidance for both kids and parents alike and reinforces how we can shine God's light through our actions, words, and choices."

Melissa S. Miller

Growing God's Fruit is a book that not only addresses the spiritual development of children, but also meets academic objectives and addresses the acquisition of life skills for all people. Academically, this book allows students of all ages to practice reading comprehension by learning new vocabulary and by making connections to the world and themselves. In addition, the vocabulary builds language development and an understanding of science standards. Another significant focus in education right now is on children's mental health, or life skills. Growing God's Fruit allows children a concrete way to practice choosing one's own thoughts, choosing the social media content in which to partake, and growing perseverance as they practice the Fruits of the Spirit in their everyday lives. Growing healthy habits of mind takes time and perseverance; comparing these habits of mind with the growth of an apple tree provides students with a concrete model on which to base their practices.

J. Ferris, Elementary Principal

FAITHFULNESS

LOVE   JOY   PEACE

SELF-CONTROL

PATIENCE

KINDNESS

Dedicated to
Our Lord and Savior, Jesus Christ, all His children, and my
special young friend, Evie, for her contributions.

*"And whatever you do, whether in word or deed, do
it all in the name of the Lord Jesus, giving thanks to
God the Father through Him."* Colossians 3:17

GENTLENESS

GOODNESS

FAITHFULNESS

"But the fruit of the Spirit is love, joy, peace, forbearance, kindness, goodness, faithfulness, gentleness, and self-control. Against such things there is no law."

Galatians 5:22-23

LOVE   JOY   PEACE

SELF-CONTROL

KINDNESS

Welcome to my garden. I plant many healthy things in my garden. I want to teach you how I care for my apple trees from tiny seeds to delicious apples.

How I plant my apple seeds and care for them reminds me of how God plants spiritual seeds in our hearts and minds, and we need to care for them, so we produce good fruit.

I am the gardener of my apple trees. God is the gardener of our minds and hearts. God helps us grow **spiritual** fruit like love, joy, peace, patience, kindness, goodness, faithfulness, gentleness, and self-control.

GENTLENESS

GOODNESS

FAITHFULNESS

"So then, just as you received Christ Jesus as Lord, continue to live your lives in him, rooted and built up in him, strengthened in the faith as you were taught, and overflowing with thankfulness."

Colossians 2:6-7

SELF-CONTROL

PATIENCE

KINDNESS

GENTLENESS

GOODNESS

Apple trees are **deciduous**, flowering fruit trees that grow from tiny seeds I plant and care for every day. If I take good care of them and make sure they have plenty of sunshine, they will grow delicious fruit for us to enjoy.

If we take care of our spiritual seeds, they grow roots in God. We grow our spiritual seeds by practicing what the Bible teaches us and by talking to God.

FAITHFULNESS

"But the seed falling on good soil refers to someone who hears the word and understands it. This is the one who produces a crop, yielding a hundred, sixty or thirty times what was sown."

Matthew 13:23

LOVE　　JOY　　PEACE

SELF-CONTROL

KINDNESS

Before I plant my apple seeds, I **cultivate** the soil to get it ready for planting. When I **cultivate** the soil, I get rid of all the weeds and turn the soil over with my shovel to loosen it up. When I plant my apple seeds in the cultivated ground, the water and air can easily flow through the dirt to the seeds so they can grow.

We must also **cultivate** our hearts and minds so we can grow spiritual fruit. We cultivate our spiritual seeds by spending time with Jesus so we can become more like Him.

GENTLENESS

GOODNESS

FAITHFULNESS

"So neither the one who plants nor the one who waters is anything, but only God, who makes things grow."

I Corinthians 3:7

SELF-CONTROL

PATIENCE

KINDNESS

GENTLENESS

GOODNESS

When I plant apple trees from seeds, it can take almost 10 years before I can harvest apples to eat. Apple trees grow very slowly and sometimes I can't even see their growth. I just care for them every day and be patient while they grow.

Apple trees don't grow overnight and neither do we. We need to be patient and **commit** to read our Bible and talk with God every day. It takes us many years of slow and steady growth to become more like Jesus.

"The one who sowed the good seed is the Son of Man. The field is the world, and the good seed stands for the people of the kingdom. The weeds are the people of the evil one, and the enemy who sows them is the devil."

Matthew 13:37-39

SELF-CONTROL

KINDNESS

GENTLENESS

GOODNESS

For apple trees to grow, we need to get rid of the weeds near the apple seedlings. The weeds steal the seedling's **nutrients** and water and make them weak and their growth slow. Apple seedlings that are choked out with weeds cannot produce apples, so I need to root out the weeds.

The Bible teaches us that we have worldly weeds that choke out our spirit's growth and we need to root out those weeds, so they do not slow our spiritual growth. Weeds that slow our growth could be jealousy, anger, selfishness, pride, greed, and lying. Weeds could also be activities or people that pull us away from God.

We need to get rid of the weeds.

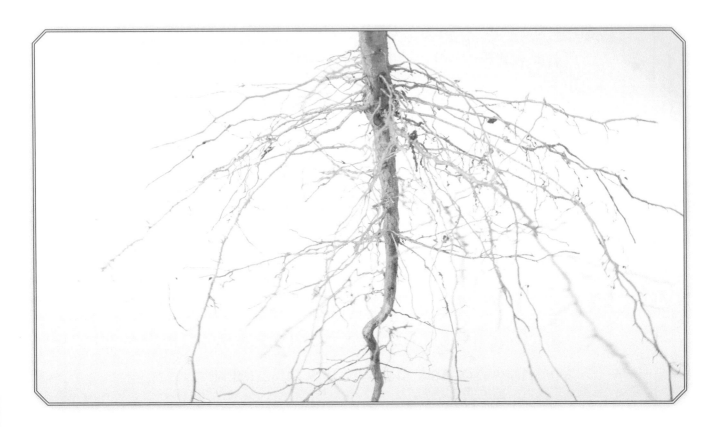

"The seed falling on rocky ground refers to someone who hears the word and at once receives it with joy. ²¹But since they have no root, they last only a short time. When trouble or persecution comes because of the word, they quickly fall away."

Matthew 13: 20-21

SELF-CONTROL

GENTLENESS

KINDNESS

GOODNESS

Apple trees have a deep taproot that grows straight into the ground and many fibrous roots that grow **horizontal** and spread around the apple tree. The taproot anchors the young apple tree into the soil until the shallower **horizontal fibrous** root system grows strong and secures the apple tree.

Deep roots in Jesus allow us to be strong and secure. Our roots grow deeper when we learn from the Bible, spend time with God in prayer, and spend time with others who have deep roots in Jesus. If we are not anchored in the good soil of what the Bible teaches us, we will have shallow roots and struggle to survive life's troubles.

"And let us consider how we may spur one another on toward love and good deeds, not giving up meeting together, as some are in the habit of doing, but encouraging one another..."

Hebrews 10:24-25

SELF-CONTROL

GENTLENESS

PATIENCE

KINDNESS

GOODNESS

Apple trees must be planted in pairs or big groups. They need each other to produce fruit. They often grow in orchards with lots of other apple trees nearby which makes it easier for the bees to do their **pollination** work so fruit can be produced. I'll tell you about **pollination** in a minute.

Just like the apple trees help each other produce beautiful fruit, surrounding ourselves with other Christians helps us grow in our faith and produce beautiful **spiritual** fruit. God will often use one person to help another person grow.

God also gave us a Helper named the Holy Spirit that came to live in us when we accepted Jesus. The Holy Spirit waters our spiritual seeds by helping us understand God's word and training us to practice what we learn so we can grow beautiful fruit.

"All Scripture is God-breathed and is useful for teaching, rebuking, correcting and training in righteousness,[17] *so that the servant of God*[a] *may be thoroughly equipped for every good work."*

2 Timothy 3:16-17

SELF-CONTROL

KINDNESS

Spring is a busy time for my apple trees. They sprout new branches and new buds. The shoots grow quickly. My apple trees look beautiful in their spring blossoms.

The center of each blossom is filled with yummy **nectar** that bees in my neighborhood enjoy drinking. The bees have an important job to do. I don't need to do anything special to invite the bees to visit, they just show up every spring.

Jesus is our great gardener and grows spiritual fruit in us when we stay connected to Him. Reading and thinking about the Bible and letting the Holy Spirit work will grow our fruit.

GENTLENESS

GOODNESS

FAITHFULNESS

"I am the vine; you are the branches. If you remain in me and I in you, you will bear much fruit; apart from me you can do nothing."

John 15:5

SELF-CONTROL

KINDNESS

Here come the bees!

Their special job is to be **pollinators**. They drink the flower's nectar and as they feed, the pollen of the flower attaches to them. As they fly from tree to tree, the pollen is transferred to the **stigma** of other flowers on different trees. That's how the flowers get **fertilized**. Now the apple begins to grow. Without the **pollinators** doing their job in the spring, we would not have apples to enjoy in the fall.

Apart from Jesus, we are like **unpollinated** apple blossoms. It is impossible to produce spiritual fruit if we are separated from God. Just like the apple blossom pollen attaches to the **pollinators**, we need to stay attached to Jesus so that He can produce fruit in us.

GENTLENESS

GOODNESS

"May the God of hope fill you with all joy and peace as you trust in him, so that you may overflow with hope by the power of the Holy Spirit."

Romans 15:13

SELF-CONTROL

KINDNESS

GENTLENESS

GOODNESS

It's summer and the **fertilized** flowers grow into little green apples. The center develops first, creating the apple's core. The **outer** wall develops into the part of the apple we eat. The fruit gradually grows larger, and the small green apples begin changing color.

Our **spiritual** fruit starts small too. For us to grow the fruit of the Spirit, we need to obey the Holy Spirit who lives in us when we belong to Jesus. The Holy Spirit is a gift that God gives us to grow our fruit and share it with others.

FAITHFULNESS

"The Lord will guide you always; he will satisfy your needs in a sun-scorched land and will strengthen your frame. You will be like a well-watered garden, like a spring whose waters never fail."

Isaiah 58:11

SELF-CONTROL

KINDNESS

The apples that we **harvest** in the fall develop from faithful care and patience. We can't enjoy the delicious apples in the **harvest** without the long growing season. Apples come once a year, but the growth seasons between the fall harvests are just as important in growing apples.

Just as the beautiful blossoms and apples come and go with each growing cycle, the beautiful moments in your life will come and go too. The moments in between the beautiful ones are just as important in your growing cycle.

GENTLENESS

GOODNESS

FAITHFULNESS

"He cuts off every branch in me that bears no fruit, while every branch that does bear fruit he prunes so that it will be even more fruitful."

John 15:2

SELF-CONTROL

KINDNESS

In late winter, I need to prune my trees, so they grow well and produce good apples. The best time to clean and **prune** apple trees is late in the winter because that is when the tree is **dormant**. It is like giving the tree a haircut while it is asleep and not actively growing.

I clean my apple trees by removing branches that look dead to keep the tree healthy. Sick branches steal **nutrients** from the tree. I also **prune** some of the branches from the tree so the sun can shine into the tree and help the apples ripen next season.

We are like the branches on God's tree. God will clean away the things about us that are not producing fruit. God **prunes** away sins and distractions that are slowing our **spiritual** growth. When we accept God's **pruning**, we will produce new growth and overflowing fruits of the Spirit.

GENTLENESS

GOODNESS

A good tree cannot bear bad fruit, and a bad tree cannot bear good fruit.

Matthew 7:18

LOVE   JOY   PEACE

SELF-CONTROL

KINDNESS

When the apples are ripe and ready, we eat them. When our spiritual fruit is ready in our minds and hearts, it needs to make its way to the outside through how we act and what we say.

Just like the apples that we grow and eat can spoil, the fruit of the Spirit is also **perishable**. It's beautiful to look at but it must be shared with others, or it will spoil.

GENTLENESS

GOODNESS

FAITHFULNESS

"Do not be deceived: God cannot be mocked. A man reaps what he sows. [8] Whoever sows to please their flesh, from the flesh will reap destruction; whoever sows to please the Spirit, from the Spirit will reap eternal life."

Galatians 6:7-9

LOVE JOY PEACE

SELF-CONTROL

PATIENCE

KINDNESS

GENTLENESS

GOODNESS

All seeds that I plant bring some kind of harvest. If I plant apple seeds, I will harvest delicious apples. If I plant flower seeds, I will get a harvest of beautiful flowers. If I plant weed seeds, I will get a weed harvest.

All our words, thoughts, and actions are the seeds we plant. If we plant seeds of love, we will harvest love. If we plant seeds of anger, we will grow anger. If we plant seeds of kindness, we will receive kindness in return.

FAITHFULNESS

"In the same way, let your light shine before others, that they may
see your good deeds and glorify your Father in heaven."

Matthew 5:16

LOVE   JOY   PEACE

SELF-CONTROL

KINDNESS

What seeds are you planting?

Are you practicing thoughts and actions that grow love, joy, peace, patience, kindness, goodness, faithfulness, gentleness, and self-control? If you **nurture** seeds that produce the fruits of the Spirit, you will grow healthy fruits.

Are you getting rid of the weedy sin in your life so you can grow in Christ?

These are the things that help others and show others that Jesus lives in us.

Colossians 2:6-7

GENTLENESS

GOODNESS

FAITHFULNESS

"If you then...know how to give good gifts to your children, how much more will your Father in heaven give the Holy Spirit to those who ask him!"

Luke 11:13

SELF-CONTROL

GENTLENESS

KINDNESS

GOODNESS

God fills everyone who asks with His Spirit. When the Holy Spirit lives inside you, spiritual seeds have been planted. The Holy Spirit lives in you to teach you what you need to produce good fruit and to lead you to God's plan for your life.

When you grow your spiritual fruit and let it **mature**, you can use the gifts that God has given you in a powerful way.

How can you grow love, joy, peace, patience, kindness, goodness, faithfulness, gentleness, and self-control in your life? If you need a little help, ask God and His Spirit will help you!

GLOSSARY

In order they appear in the book:

Spiritual	-relating to the spirit
Deciduous	-leaves falling off seasonally
Cultivate	-to prepare for raising crops
Commit	-to pledge or obligate oneself
Nutrients	-substance that promotes growth and provides energy
Horizontally	-parallel to the horizon
Fibrous	-stringy fibers
Pollination	-the transfer of pollen from plant anther to the plant stigma
Nectar	-a sweet liquid secreted by a plant
Stigma	-the sticky part of the plant where pollen germinates
Pollinators	-one that pollinates flowers
Unpollinated	-something that has not been pollinated
Fertilized	-to cause a seed to develop into a new young plant
Outer	-being away from the center
Harvest	-the season for gathering crops
Prune	-to cut back parts
Dormant	-asleep; inactive
Perishable	-likely to spoil or decay
Nurture	-feed and nourish
Mature	-grown to a final, desired state

LOVE   JOY   PEACE

SELF-CONTROL

PATIENCE

ACTIVITIES

1. Divide your paper in half, on the left side write one Fruit of the Spirit, and on the right side write down or draw pictures of three ways you can demonstrate that Fruit of the Spirit.

2. Create a custom illustrated bookmark including drawings and words from your favorite Fruit of the Spirit.

3. Create a "most wanted" poster of the Fruit of the Spirit that you most want to see demonstrated by others. Remember to include why that Fruit is wanted.

4. Vocabulary Dice Game (on following page)

KINDNESS

GOODNESS

GENTLENESS

FAITHFULNESS

SELF-CONTROL

PATIENCE

KINDNESS

GOODNESS

GENTLENESS

 VOCABULARY DICE FUN

Dice makes learning new vocabulary words fun. Using standard dice, roll one die for each word found in **bold** print in the book. Do the activity according to what number is rolled.

1 – Give a definition in your own words

2 – Give a synonym & antonym

3 – Draw a picture

4 – Use the word in your own sentence

5 – Tell someone about your new word

6 – Your choice

Rolling the die makes it FUN! Use a separate piece of paper to record your roll. Choose two or three words each time you read the book or complete the entire list.

AN APPLE OBJECT LESSON

Adults may follow the numbered procedure below while reading the bold text aloud to their child. This object lesson reinforces the message of the book about surrounding ourselves with other Christians to help produce beautiful spiritual fruit.

Materials needed: Apple, vinegar, sugar, cinnamon, two baggies, knife for slicing

We learned in our book that just like the apple trees help each other produce beautiful fruit, surrounding ourselves with other Christians helps us grow in our faith and produce beautiful spiritual fruit.

1. Slice the apple into slices.
2. Divide your apple slices into two baggies and label them with their team names: "The Bittersweets" and "Happily Ever Apples."

Meet The Bittersweets team. They are a group of apples that look sweet but are really not very sweet. They are not kind to others. They do not use "please" and "thank you." They are not patient and sometimes say mean things about others. That makes them kind of bitter.

3. Pour drops of vinegar into The Bittersweets baggie. Ask your child smell and describe it.)

The Bittersweets did not obey or respect their parents and teachers.

4. Pour a few more drops of vinegar into The Bittersweets baggie and let your child smell it. By now The Bittersweets should be in a puddle of vinegar in the baggie.

The Bible tells us that "bad company corrupts good character." (I Corinthians 15:33) Before long all of the children on Team Bittersweet were bitter, disrespectful and behaving badly. Do you want to sample the apples on Team Bittersweet? Do you want to join Team Bittersweet? Why?

Now meet the "Happily Ever Apples" team. They are a group of friends who all look sweet, and they all act very sweet. They show patience and love to others.

5. Sprinkle some sugar and cinnamon in the "Happily Ever Apples" baggie and let your child smell it and describe it.

The Happily Ever Apples team remember to say "please" and "thank you" and are respectful to their parents and teachers. They are polite and always lend a helping hand to those in need.

6. Sprinkle more sugar and cinnamon in the "Happily Ever Apples" baggies and shake it up to coat the apple slices.

Would you like to sample the apples on Team Happily Ever Apple? Do you want to join Team Happily Ever After? Why? What kind of friend do you want to be: one that makes everyone bitter or one that is sweet? What can you do to show sweet fruit?

About the Author

G.H. Servant is the author's pen name for God's Humble Servant. G.H. Servant's mission is to bring children and their parents into God's Kingdom. G.H. Servant accepts no profits from the sale of books and donates proceeds back to the mission to the glory of God.

Printed in the United States
by Baker & Taylor Publisher Services